Connect Like You Did When You First Met

101 Proven Questions for Couples

by Tony & Alisa DiLorenzo

ONE Extraordinary Marriage
13960 Carmel Ridge Road
San Diego, CA 92128
(858)876-5663

Ordering Information:

Quantity sales. Special discounts are available on quantity purchases by corporations, associations, and others. For details, contact authors at the address above.

Connect Like You Did When Your First Met:
101 Proven Questions for Couples

Printed in the United States of America

Table of Contents

Special Bonus Offer

As a thank you for purchasing this book, you are invited to download exclusive content including:

Connect Like You Did When You First Met eBook (PDF)
4 Quick Tips to Improved Communication Checklist (PDF)
Audio #1 - The Choices You Make Every Day (mp3)
Audio #2 - I'm Sorry (mp3)
Audio #3 - Want To or Need To (mp3)
Audio #4 - To Text or Not To Text (mp3)

Get your bonuses by visiting
ConnectLikeYouDidBonus.com

Revive Your Communication and Your Marriage

Husbands and wives don't think alike all the time. Do you agree with us?

Because the two of you don't think exactly alike it is not uncommon for you and your spouse to be on different playing fields when it comes to your communication styles. Your upbringing, life experiences, how long you've been married, stress, kids and many other factors have brought you to this point

By reviving your communication and connecting in a way you haven't in the past will keep the flames of love, laughter, and intimacy in your marriage growing each and every week, month and year that passes.

Your communication styles may be impacting you more than you realize right now. If so, you and your spouse need to take time to revive your emotional intimacy starting today!

To do this both of you need to be patient with each other and persistent to learning how each of you communicates. It's going to take work on both of your parts to learn how to communicate effectively. It doesn't happen overnight and it won't get better if you don't start from where you are right now.

Get ready because it is time to revive the emotional intimacy your marriage.

You will find that by asking and answering questions the two of you will increase your connection with each other. As the connection heightens this will for sure spill over to other areas of your marriage.

Five years ago we started implementing each of these skills into our marriage. We're so thrilled that we have because after 18 years of marriage we are closer emotionally, spiritually and sexually than ever before.

Schedule Time to Talk

This is of the highest priority! Both of you need to choose a time during your week when it best suited for both of you. Don't try and do this right before bed when you are tired or when a football game is on.

Set yourselves up for success.

You both may need to get up early in the morning, after the kids go to bed, or while taking a drive on the weekend. Write these dates on your calendar and keep to them. You wouldn't back out on a meeting at work would you?

Grow Your Communication Skills

We commend you because you are doing just that. Reading books, listening to audio programs, podcasts, watching videos, or hiring a coach are all ways that you can expand your communication skills.

Some of the techniques you will try will work wonderfully and others will not. Move forward with what does and continue to learn new ways to increase your emotional intimacy.

Listen More Than You Talk

There are times when you need to remember that you were given two ears for a reason. The reason being that you should listen twice as much as you are talking. Be an active listener during this time.

Don't look at your phone, or iPad, computer, Kindle, or anything else for that matter. Put all of your attention into your spouse so that they know you are interested in what is happening with them.

One Question at a Time

Stick to one question per session. We know this can be tough and yet when the both of you focus in on one question each of you will be more engaged. Jumping from question to question will cause your spouse to disengage and zone out quicker than you can get your point across.

Stay focused. You can do it!

Keep it Short and Simple

When the conversation goes on and on and on your spouse may begin to zone out. This isn't a good place to be when you're reviving your communication. You may be like the Energizer Bunny (going on and on and on) and your spouse is completely lost.

It is during these times that you need to catch yourself and quickly make your point. As a spouse this is a time to ask nicely for your spouse to make their point so that you can complete the question. Stay focused on the question as you clearly share your thoughts.

Body Language Speaks Volumes

Take stock of how you have positioned yourself. Your non-verbal cues speak loud and clear to your spouse if you are engaged in the conversation or not.

Are your arms crossed? Are you avoiding eye contact? Are you pacing around? These and other ways your express yourself through your body language will hinder your ability to connect with your spouse as you go through these questions.

Use "I" Statements to Express Yourself

Do you want your spouse to get defensive and check out of while you are going over these questions? If you do then use "You" statements. You statements put your spouse on the defense and they are quick to defend their stance.

Statements such as, "You never listen to me" or "Why can't you..." would put you on your heals, right?

Instead turn these statements to "I" statement. An example of this is, "I get irritated when we talk because I need your full attention".

This is one of the tougher ones in our opinion. Work on rewording how you speak to your spouse. If you need to, write down what you want to say so that it comes out clearly.

Encourage One Another

Learning a skill such as communicating better together takes time and encouragement. Make it a point to tell each other how opening up and sharing deep intimate issues are helping to foster a stronger bond.

Don't forget to use other forms of communications, letters, text, email, etc after you've answered a question(s) that brought the two of you closer. Doing this will encourage your spouse and will keep them coming back for more.

Take each of these suggestions and begin practicing them regularly when the two of you are answering the questions below. Not only is the deeper emotional connection going to prosper, but the time together will overflow into all areas of your marriage.

101 Proven Questions for Couples

Our Marriage

— Question 1 —

What can I do to communicate my love and appreciation to you?

— Question 2 —

Is there anything you need from me that you're not getting?

— Question 3 —

What is one specific way that I can be a better spouse to you?

— Question 4 —

What can we do to stay focused on the foundation of our marriage?

— Question 5 —

When does opening up to me seem risky to you?

— Question 6 —

What victories do you think have built up our marriage?

— Question 7 —

What five things can you always count on me for?

— Question 8 —

What are some personal issues you have faced in your life, that have impacted our marriage?

— Question 9 —

What lessons did you learn from your parents about marriage?

— Question 10 —

What is one of the most romantic times we've had together?

— Question 11 —

What are three qualities you most admire in me?

Let's Talk About Sex

— Question 12 —

What are you most concerned about in our sex life?

— Question 13 —

On a scale of
(1-the lowest to 10-the highest)
How important is sex to you?
and why?

— Question 14 —

When we have problems in our sex life, what way(s) would you like to address them?

— Question 15 —

What does foreplay mean to you?

— Question 16 —

What touches stimulate you sexually?

— Question 17 —

Where would you like
to have sex?
(Any location either in our
house or out of it)

— Question 18 —

Do you ever had erotic thoughts about me?
Describe them.

— Question 19 —

How can I respond to you sexually during your period? Is sex an option or are there other things we can do?

— Question 20 —

What is outside your comfort zone in bed?

— Question 21 —

On a scale of
(1-the lowest to 10-the highest)
What is your comfort level when
it comes to oral sex?
Answer for both giving and
receiving.

— Question 22 —

Where, on your body, are the 3 favorite places for me to kiss you?

Dollars and Sense

— Question 23 —

What do you want to do during our retirement?

— Question 24 —

How much do you want to save for retirement?

— Question 25 —

What changes do you feel we need make to our finances so we are on the same page?

— Question 26 —

What were you taught as a child about finances?

— Question 27 —

How would you feel if I made more money than you?

— Question 28 —

If I wanted to go back to school or start my own business, what changes do you think we would need to make in our financial plan?

— Question 29 —

Do you think money is a big deal to you?

— Question 30 —

What does money mean to you?

— Question 31 —

What strategies can we use to pay off our debt as a team?

— Question 32 —

Are you comfortable talking about money? Why or why not?

— Question 33 —

What do you think have been our biggest struggles financially?

Spiritual Matters

— Question 34 —

What one thing have you learned about God or your faith this past year?

— Question 35 —

What hardships has God used in our lives to grow our marriage?

— Question 36 —

How do we put God at the center of our relationship?

— Question 37 —

How would you describe our spiritual life as a couple?

— Question 38 —

What scripture do you use during rough times in our marriage?

— Question 39 —

How can I encourage each other
you in your walk with God?

— Question 40 —

What do you believe to be your spiritual gifts?

— Question 41 —

When in your life you have been "on fire" for God (or passionate)? What changed?

— Question 42 —

What have you been asking God for in prayer recently?

— Question 43 —

What is your favorite scripture about marriage?

— Question 44 —

Do you see me growing more godly as the years go on? How are you measuring that?

— Question 45 —

When have you struggled with your faith?
How have you worked through that?

Dating One Another

— Question 46 —

What do you consider a fun date night?

— Question 47 —

What is YOUR definition of camping?

— Question 48 —

What activities can we do as a couple?

— Question 49 —

What new activities would you like to try?

— Question 50 —

Where have you always dreamed of visiting? Cities? Countries?

— Question 51 —

What does a spontaneous date look like to you?

Special Bonus Offer

As a thank you for purchasing this book, you are invited to download exclusive content including:

Connect Like You Did When You First Met eBook (PDF)
4 Quick Tips to Improved Communication Checklist (PDF)
Audio #1 - The Choices You Make Every Day (mp3)
Audio #2 - I'm Sorry (mp3)
Audio #3 - Want To or Need To (mp3)
Audio #4 - To Text or Not To Text (mp3)

Get your bonuses by visiting
ConnectLikeYouDidBonus.com

— Question 52 —

Do you like to stay home and watch a movie or go to the theater? Why?

— Question 53 —

What activities did we do together, before we got married, that you would like to do again?

— Question 54 —

What is your favorite way to exercise?

— Question 55 —

Are you open to working out together?

— Question 56 —

What ideas do you have for a date that doesn't cost us anything?

— Question 57 —

What would be the most extravagant date that we could plan?

Kids, Those Other People In Our House

— Question 58 —

How do you want to talk to our kids about sex?

— Question 59 —

What image of marriage do you want our children to have as they grow up?

— Question 60 —

Did you ever see your parents deal with conflict/ have disagreements? Are you comfortable with our own kids seeing that side of marriage?

— Question 61 —

What strategies should we use to teach our kids about money?

— Question 62 —

Where are your priorities in regard to me and the kids? Who comes first? Why?

— Question 63 —

Are kids activities more important than date nights?

— Question 64 —

How can we present a united front to our children?

— Question 65 —

What life skills do you want our kids to have as they grow into adults?

— Question 66 —

What can we do to prepare for being empty nesters?

— Question 67 —

What adjustments do we need to make to our marriage now that we have children?

— Question 68 —

What aspects of my personality have you discovered since we had kids?

— Question 69 —

How can we pray for our children?

Friends and Family

— Question 70 —

How do you feel about my interactions with your family? What could I do to make that relationship stronger?

— Question 71 —

How would you feel about my parents coming to live with us if they needed to be cared for? What challenges would you anticipate? What benefits?

— Question 72 —

Do you think I spend too much time or not enough time with my friends?

— Question 73 —

What challenges do we have with boundaries between ourselves and our parents?

— Question 74 —

In what ways do you see my friends supportive of our relationship?

— Question 75 —

In what situations do I demonstrate that you come before my family and my friends?

— Question 76 —

Do you feel like I put our relationship ahead of my relationship with my parents?

— Question 77 —

How do you feel about me having friends of the opposite sex?

— Question 78 —

How do you feel about me going out on girls night/guys night? Are there any activities that you wouldn't want me to participate in?

Dreams and Desires

— Question 79 —

What would you do if you found out you only had one day left to live?

— Question 80 —

What would be one change in my life that you most believe would be for my own good?

— Question 81 —

If there were no limitations, where do you see yourself in 5 years? Our marriage?

— Question 82 —

What are three goals you have had for over a year?

— Question 83 —

If you could open any business,
what would it be?

— Question 84 —

If you could start a non-profit or service project, what would it be?

— Question 85 —

If you were given 1 million dollars every month, and the only thing you had to do was give, who would you give it to? (Excludes family and friends)

— Question 86 —

Where would you live if you could live anywhere in the world?

— Question 87 —

If you became famous, how would you live your life differently?

— Question 88 —

What does success mean to you?

— Question 89 —

Before you die, what would you like to have accomplished?

— Question 90 —

If you could do what you have always dreamed of doing, what would it be?

Rapid Fire

— Question 91 —

If you had to give yourself a nickname, what would it be?

— Question 92 —

If you were to give me a nickname, what would it be?

— Question 93 —

The most embarrassing thing that ever happened to you was...

— Question 94 —

What is your favorite genre of music? Your favorite song?

— Question 95 —

Would your rather eat a cooked frog or live bugs?

— Question 96 —

Would you rather never have to clean the kitchen again, or never clean the bathroom again?

— Question 97 —

What is the movie title or song that best sums up our sex life?

— Question 98 —

If you had to describe my kiss as a food, what would it be and why?

— Question 99 —

Would you rather trip and fall in front of ten people you don't know, or say something embarrassing in front of one celebrity? Why?

— Question 100 —

If you were to be on a reality TV show, which one would you want to be on?

— Question 101 —

If you had to restart your life, what age would your start from?

Special Bonus Offer

As a thank you for purchasing this book, you are invited to download exclusive content including:

Connect Like You Did When You First Met eBook (PDF)
4 Quick Tips to Improved Communication Checklist (PDF)
Audio #1 - The Choices You Make Every Day (mp3)
Audio #2 - I'm Sorry (mp3)
Audio #3 - Want To or Need To (mp3)
Audio #4 - To Text or Not To Text (mp3)

Get your bonuses by visiting
ConnectLikeYouDidBonus.com

Bonus Questions

1. How would you describe the word "love"?
2. Would you prefer ice cubes or hot wax during sex? Why?
3. Have you ever felt bored with our marriage? What were the circumstances? What changed so that you no longer feel that way?
4. What were your goals for our marriage when we were engaged? What are they now?
5. What is your dream career? How can I help you achieve that goal?
6. What sexual desires, do you have, that we haven't discussed?
7. In what ways am I the ideal spouse for you?
8. What is a current source of stress for you? How can I help you through this?
9. How can I challenge your thinking without crushing your dreams?
10. What things in our marriage make you happy? sad?
11. What do you think your purpose in life is?
12. Where do I instinctively turn when things are challenging in our marriage?
13. Do you enjoy phone sex with me?

14. What do you think our marriage will be like when we are older?
15. How should decisions about managing our home be made?
16. If you were having problems sexually (struggles with performance, low libido, etc.) would you prefer to talk to me about it first or with your doctor?
17. How are we grounded in our marriage? What is our foundation built on?
18. In what way would you like to grow this year?
19. What caresses do you enjoy the most? the least?
20. What are the 3 biggest lessons you have learned from previous relationships?
21. Which do you prefer...Owning a home or renting? Why?
22. What has been the toughest experience of your life?
23. What do you believe it takes to have a good marriage?
24. What distractions keep us from spending time with one another?
25. What are your weaknesses?

26. When did you first notice me? What was the attraction?
27. Do we work together spiritually to your satisfaction? How can we become stronger in this area?
28. What are your fears when it comes to being married?
29. What boundaries should we have in our marriage (kids, work, parents, friends, phones, social media)?
30. Thrift store shopping: great deals or gross? Why?
31. How can I be a better spouse to you?
32. What do you most wish we could do to make an impact on the world for Christ?
33. What would you do if you had to live on a mountain or an island without warning?
34. What charities do you feel inspired to support? How can we get more involved with them?
35. What was your most fulfilling moment in our marriage this past year?
36. What would you do with $1 million, $5 million, $10 million?

37. How are we overcommitted to stuff/other activities and not committed to one another?
38. Saving money is easy/hard for me because...
39. What worries you most about life?
40. Why did you marry me?
41. What kind of small gifts or acts can I give you to let you know how much I appreciate you?
42. Spending money is easy/hard for me because…
43. What has helped you grow in your walk with God in the last 12 months?
44. What is your favorite scripture and why?
45. What one aspect or thing in your life are you most encouraged about or thankful for right now?
46. What ways can we build our friendship more?
47. What are your favorite worship songs?
48. Do I sometimes embarrass you?
49. What is your favorite book of the bible?
50. What is your definition of communication?
51. If I were to become disabled or seriously ill, how do you think you would handle that? What would be the most difficult aspects?

52. What scripture best describes our marriage?
53. How do you feel about being affectionate in front of our children?
54. Do you feel I have an "on-fire" attitude for our marriage? Why or why not?
55. Do you think a Proverbs 31 wife is an ideal wife? Why or why not?
56. In the past 6 months what has been your most encouraging experience? Discouraging?

Love You Guys

Tony and Alisa have been married for 18 years and not all of them have been happy ones. Like you, they came together with every good intention and "forever" in mind, but then "life" happened and they found themselves ill prepared to deal with their marriage challenges.

Not only were they struggling as a couple, but they were also both struggling with their own personal hurdles independent of one another. Their "bumps in the road" were actually mountains in their eyes and they knew that in order to get to the other side, keep their family together, and experience a loving, intimate marriage, they were going to need to dig deep and address their circumstances head-on.

Dealing with it all was their commitment to each other. Together, they overcame Tony's 18-year addiction to pornography, the loss of a child at 18 weeks, debt in excess of $50,000, poor communication, lack of collective interests, and questioning trust. But, the key word here is "together".

They have learned some hard knock life lessons and have discovered key principles that have kept their marriage (and sex life) alive and flourishing… and they did it together. You can do the same!

Love you guys,

Tony & Alisa DiLorenzo

He Zigs, She Zags: Get Your Communication on the Same Path

The ability to talk to each other is vital to all areas of your marriage. Here's the thing...if there is unease when talking, tension or bickering you know the stress that it places on you. You're drained.

This isn't good for you, your spouse or your kids (if you have kids).

It's time to get your communication on the same path with your spouse.

It's time to take control of the communication in your marriage. There is so much that is happening in your life each and every day that if you do not take the time to learn how to best connect with your spouse you are going to struggle for years to come.

He Zigs, She Zags **will equip you to honor your spouse through effective communication** in a fun, loving environment. In this program you'll learn how to rock your communication and your sex life.

Learn more about He Zigs, She Zags today at www.HeZigsSheZags.com